HUNTING IS PAINTING

First published 2010 by &NOW Books, an imprint of Lake Forest College Press.

Directors   Associate Director
Robert Archambeau   Joshua Corey
Davis Schneiderman

Box A-16
Lake Forest College
555 N. Sheridan Road
Lake Forest, IL 60045

lakeforest.edu/andnow

Cover image by Allison Hawkins, *Friends,* 2007. Ink and watercolor on paper.
Interior images by Allison Hawkins, 2010. Ink on paper.

Lake Forest College Press, based at Chicago's National Liberal Arts College, publishes in the broad spaces of Chicago studies. Our imprint, &NOW Books, publishes innovative and conceptual literature and serves as the publishing arm of the &NOW writers' conference and organization.

&Now Executive Board:
Steve Tomasula, Founder
Dimitri Anastasopoulos
Robert Archambeau
Rebecca Goodman
Christina Milletti
Martin Nakell
Davis Schneiderman

ISBN-13: 978-0-9823156-2-0
ISBN-10: 0-9823156-2-7

Book design by Emma Therieau

Printed in the United States

For my dear parents

and in memory of
Preble Corine Daniels and Carolyn D'Orsogna

CONTENTS

YOUR LITTLE OAR CHIPPED THE SEA

THE RIB'S GREY RAINBOW EVOKES FIDELITY

FIRE IS THE STATUE WITH THE YOUNG FACE

I SEND OUT AN ISOSCELES TRIANGLE
TO THE BIRDS AND FISH

CONCEPTION IS THE BREAKING CHAIN
OF A BURNING TORCH

DEATH AND LIFE AS SNODGRASS AND CLEO
EQUALING
THE LOVE POEMS OF SNODGRASS AND CLEO

IN THE PARVIS THE GREEN WREATH
REASSEMBLED

YOUR LITTLE OAR
CHIPPED THE SEA

IN THE BAND OF PAINTERS AND PHOTOGRAPHERS
HIRED TO DETERMINE THE FERTILITY OF AMERICA

Bats drizzling in twilight
stripes of circus canopy on the tiger's belly
I put my face near the soil sample and hear
the dirt dreaming of trumpet vine and a city garden with cotton candy
and a zoo with little signs by the animals
the dirt I try to extract from the paint is part of the paint

my eyes closed and laughing and the prince-cook
at the campfire makes me meat I can taste the field in
I thought, "gun as microscope"

the river stands up for a moment and the fish rest on rocks
and I go homeward and found a park in the woods
and the pond is one wave I can spear

> I see my wife standing there
> I said, the tree is filling out in leaves
> don't stand behind that tree
> I can see your eye, loved-one
> but soon the tree is filled out in leaves

Hunting Is Painting

Brown shirt littered in dove's blood;
Hunting is painting and excavating some greater forest.
And hose-water and knife through scales
Cooks alcohol of supper—
I spread the light in salt over my food
And often use a knife to remove a bruise
From the golden peach.

There is bait in the mouths of ice-fishermen.

I Carry a Radio I Carry a Human Invention Strapped to My Back

    Carries the dead man
    Dead man like a machine with its wheels still spinning
    Hairs on his arms crawl back into shape
Mine my life
Mine my life, I carry you, heavy as an upturned hedge
And the radio on my back
One may carry an invention on his back
Can hear you though I am snowed in like a scenery
    Gnats glow in piles
    Telephone poles to their knees in soil, fire's arm on
    The steady shoulder of the heat
    Fleas blink itch and madness near the examination
    Between blood and air
I maneuver this or that and locate F major in landing position
Mine my life over and out into the future ear
Once we located the gun and invented a magical vanish
    Great guns and little fishes
    The voice raises itself to stand in anguish
    And pulls down a patrol car
    Her hair creaks like elevators, the age of Towers has shoved itself
    Into barrels of outdated shotguns in glass cases

The part in the death lady's hair shines out like a fishbone

    My life is the white face of a boat over the water out in waves

    Beside the figure of the brain, the radio falls in waves, all nights

Apotropaic Uniform

Let's stand together on the soft ground
I will hand you these things which will protect you on the journey
white bird has feathers as one thousand inverted ribs
he'll stand lovingly on your head, there now
hold up this vase and its small swamp
like a lantern with a dirty glow
thin piece of green foil trimmed into the shape of a sickle
and pasted to your chest
at your side the thin deer with the asshole shriveling like a rose
opera glasses dripping with paint, and
birch cane on the forearm.

You're ready to gallop into the infinite stage of a city garden.

STILL LIFE OF THE HERD

I am perfume without its bottle on! A steeple headdress
                                        you offer me?
I humiliate the grass.
No mercy for the obscene: Someday I will wear a houndstooth coat I
                        swear to Christ Almighty

I sharpen my pencil with a knife and have hugeous hands!
I wear an orange robe.
5, 679, 327 pure gold barrettes and genuine leather twigs to pin up
                        my black hair.

I read a novel and little hairs fall all over the page:
"All the animals steaming over the hill."
Will you triumph in the after-life cycle? I mean there I am
            with the other young feeding upon my own sloppy breasts.

I move through the still frozen cloud of snow.
I campaign for decadent feed.
I shower off my education.
I am the one who told them to use hammers inside the pianos. Treatment
of musical areas. Earliest popular music of all nations: Let us jump
three times as the star lands. Enough.

    People within the improved fences of picnics steeping over
    a single mountain.

THE RIB'S GREY RAINBOW
EVOKES FIDELITY

RECORDING THE VIRGINS

The violinist depends upon his own electric drawings of himself
     Pulling his bow this way and that, he is frantically
    drawing himself into being, climbing his own dizziness

Major chords march off to war.
 The triplet of three sailors on a boat, the mast, the edge, the trill:

    My dearest God, do you recall the shift from gospel
    to love songs?
    To reinvent the gospel song as love song requires
    someday the lovers write a sad song back to God:

        All the music of a thunderstorm doesn't bring you back
        All the jukeboxes in the world can't match your collection

    That's music, dove.

Earnest melody rises up from the feet of lovers
on their ways back home

    Music essentially means that you are forever
    on your way to something, whistling bird notes
                       to keep the bears away.

Before the Trees Were Young

A ship smiles backwards through unraveled storms
Rain swinging in on frozen ropes

The white paint between two waves
Splashes like torchlight

Rowing in a steady lightning, Noah fights to save the coupled waters
Each second sprouts a white hair on his nose

As the wave like a soft muscle within a shell
Outgrows its abstract space

Double arcs splash on stairs to ship—
They would have sunk the beasts and men

No evil
In this great round garden.

DESTROYING SCATHEFUL MATTER AND PURCHASING EXCELLENT MATTER

Destroying scatheful matter and purchasing excellent matter,
Preble Corine, those were the days of junk and distance
Movement from product to product
Heaven is tall, but with the everlasting posture of anti-gravity we
        will reach it yet
The hilarious shooting plane: in a gesture of measurement to the sun
Pap-Paw gropes the rifle while Nana's fur stole rides her shoulders
Grandfather buys the rifle; Nana has 8 Sears shop girls package fur
        it's all the rage
Heaven is tall but wait just a cotton-pickin' minute the field
        is the farmer or government's rising roof
The living ancestor buys shadows which are floating past the hedges
Preble my Nana she is lying lean against the yellow shop sign
        with the auburn mysticism of iced-tea
Heaven is tall, but there is paint in the life,
        dining room table rouge, the blush will not exit

Two hands rejoice in their synchronous movement to the top of the head
to fix the hat into place

Heaven is tall and dark and handsome but Preble Corine your lampshades

               so gold in laughing hats position in the storm

MOTHER IS SEWING

Ice-fishing, pulling the line into posture.
It's a lift-smoke;
fish beneath that snow-horizon
rise with her hook in threaded knots.

Paintings of ships sliding by on strings
Up to her elbows in the living waters.

And singing, she is the treble clef:

Mother with the curved center rests upon multiple horizons.

To Paint Down the Flame on a Birthday Candle Is a Symptom of Congruity

The father cuts the pear and the daughter appears.
The waker is a dream to the sun.

There are animals from children's books and from nature programs. But
animals also have a memory of the young children

                little snail appears on the sea plant
                it is very windy, leaves tend to drop—

Then after a bunch of years, Petra grows up.
        Her job is Sweeper of the Bingo Hall
            Petra you are a yellow-skirted bird
            in a theater of wood
            You are a boy in workman's pants clutching roses
            You are holding a box of fruits:
                you will expire.

Some nights you might feel like the Sky Girl at the Rust Twist Dance
        Oh and sometimes you are very sullen,
            and yet your headdress is very gay.

Will anyone adore the bearded knees of this late virgin?
The angular creep of beautiful bells in her left ear

    and the more present fly
    heat in her ears from three generations of pop songs—

When you tell her good-bye, say something like,
           "Farewell, my sweet building."

PETRA DREAMING IN HER RAINING-DOWN GRIN

You could have been a hot little breakfast
    you could have met a boy from a different tribe
    and stood up to watch the sun go down.

      The waker is a dream to the sun.

          There is the allure of a two-day pass to an open city:
          Last night, blue door and shower on
          the poor man's fireworks of wet roses

            Practice Field:

        "I do not know what I am doing out here in the rain
        Like an air conditioner surrounded by green paint."

          Movie plays itself out on the sticks in this campfire,
          ambulance lights flash in the fire-pit.
          The closet-electric sound
          of a band playing in a nearby park—
          young musicians would play fast
          young products are whole and fresh.
          You have noted the rotting in order in laundry baskets
          and the cold water splashes half-jaw
          at the drinking fountain.
          You have never been what they called pretty enough
          to be patrolled by boats

Petra's boat:

      fish oil beard, little lights scraping
      through.
      They were on the boat, floating filth
      and gun-slick water held them up

Bats Revolving Peach Blossoms

An annual dance as an old stage growing splinters,
And the backwards feeling of a tree as a rake,
Dead leaves speared into the ray of branches

> young arrangement: the nature inside your corsage,
>> makeshift bouquet of raised eyebrows
>> like curled grasses and the blushy sun

> bats revolving peach blossoms

FIRE IS THE STATUE
WITH THE YOUNG FACE

RECUERDO RADIO

Hey amorist, tune your radio to 98.6
    Above the sea-waves, beautiful and big Life
    Reportage collecting in love songs
We once discovered space is full
    of boundless sound

    Space gathers back for these new lovesome branches of singers

        We have chopped down the bunk beds of childhood
        and we have escaped the family mind. Now fully aware
        of humanity, radio and suntan oil
        and the last thing we are is tired.

The old master of landscaping certainly painted us into the rosebush!
And the gods built the beach houses, blessed be
The gods built these boats and we can sit on their laps in the sea,
and the radios with the one heavy sound for the sweet neckers
and the young boy who carries the girl into the sea.

POPULATION FIGURE

Million alarm clocks perform on bedside tables this instant
1874: two foxes mated in a railroad car
Then tender Juliet from the '60s, very affected by fissures of
       sun spots, floating island of dark hair, blond hair

       singular experience:

       Delta Motel
       brave man watches
       darting shadows of leaves
       punctuate gold drapes

Once, the machine could do anything, and Now:
       We can access any relevant fruit as it falls from our own bodies!

       We can all be magicians—
       We can make the helicopter disappear
       and tigers and dogs appear

       And no matter if you are New York
       or a great beauty
       or a can of Tab
       held in the hand of a fun-loving gal
           named Myrtle

You measure the distance from space to space.

Tina fixes her lipstick in the cheap stained glass of a novel
        and sighs, "I'm just trying to have an experience.
                Trying to record and experience

                in the exponential manner of this ocean before me,
                waves boringly drowning into one another—
                creating experience in the exponential manner of a
                                song."

Food Attitude

The fat man swimmer's heart of a honeydew melon.
You smell, snot-nosed grape. To a muffin: Bozo the Idiot.
What does an artichoke look like to an ant?
For Christ's sake, stop trying to scare
the hell out of the earth.

> Skinny girls line the balconies— they hate you.
> Fat men line your balcony— they hate you, too.
> Babies line the balcony— they cry because they cannot eat you.

You are trying to make the people look stupid
like bobbing apples with spit on red, peculiar-bitten mouths.

Sir, you had sworn off animals,
but then look at these evil strawberries on Chinette
at the nudists' picnic; hateful radishes,
the hushpuppy turns over in the skillet,
then terrified ribbons of chewing gum.

The carrot is a tap root,
yet derives from columns on antebellum houses which are fangs
that crash into the porch floor.
Haunted shaded lawns of collard greens
where a vengeful ghost steps out of her swimsuit.

> I called the fig tree a pig tree why wouldn't
> anyone tell me the truth?
> Oh little blind quadruplet lamb of cauliflowers
> with shepherdess and her dumb fish gait and stupid suicidal cane
> the drama of evangelical church cakes,
> vanilla ice cream is a pile of Christmas lights we test.

The nun in the onion: No matter how you chop you will not find
her.
Pit locked into the date.

> Bullets in the pumpkin
> Hunts Catsup of 107 cremated plastic geraniums
> I eat corn-on-the-cob. I eat my own teeth.
> I hate wet Hy-Vee produce.

> There: a lady pushes door-bell ice-cubes
> on the whiskey
> drowned ladder of mixed drinks,
> empty, hateful balloons rise
> in glasses of champagne—
> beverages:
> they self-hate because they cannot bear
> to exist outside the glass.

> We go up in airplanes to get away from vegetables
> growing aggressively, and liar fruit—
> then here comes the prison stewardesses
> strapped to their trays

> We go up to the moon!
> Freeze-dried peas float like gross
> confetti throughout the space-craft.

Home-Run pies: I buy 4 of them.
Oatmeal, you are no better than a beaten rug.
Food, you are boring and overdone— why can't the surprise girl
step out of your cake?

> You leave a shadow on the will of my mind.

> The telephone receiver of the squash—
> I speak into it and say, good-bye forever.

BUSINESS

We split the tree into pencils;
A pencil drawing of a tree makes trees angry.
There is a big color copy machine
coming out the heart of America.
Slicing a top layer of cake from the fish aquarium,
I've got lots of dreams and I'm not kidding:
garages with personal car-washes, giant sponges
squish on the lawn,
anti-gravity skating rinks with marshmallow wheels,
stereo-birthday cake with its layers of richness
and birthday song, with its lighted cracks
and static light atop each candle,
with its linear tuning across the time-line of numbers and studios
and reception and loneliness.

Scouts Learn How to Be Nurses

The director-teacher has fallen down—

Small compass by the pulse oh tell which way the body is going
Hearts hot beneath chest-horizon: thirteen tiny burning sunsets

> Birthday candle "zero" in the garden
> Pulling a sheet over the head and dying
> Family polaroid dream-shot of Great-Uncle
> taped to the head as an ancestor mask
> when attending funerals in the garden

"Madonna, You Are More Beautiful than Sunshine"
it was a smash around the campfire

we put our knapsacks in the grass

"Standing on the Promises"
let the ribbons fall in hot sand.

The Child Has a Fever the Gods Have a Fever

Fever is stained glass in the dark, and branches crack
as I pull hair away from your hot face

My golden robe smells like parade beer and fish
I call you my "little iron"
     my old back straight as a board

     A shadow hangs off the light fixture
     The stone falls off the birthday candle

You mark the darkness with little elbows
An earthquake and the plates shift in my brain—
                  you are standing at the edge
as the wave comes in. Ground pulls the tension of rain, Lucia's live
candles melt through your tantrum of hair, someone brushes out the wax;
              on each limb of your hair hangs a sun.
There you are, with school and book
learning to read and speaking from the billboards with the passion of a
     convert.

I don't know if I can heal you or keep you, I might put you under to
grow you again. I would like to try my hand at a certain distance
which keeps me from sewing needlework into the lap of my skirt.

     Fever goes to itself—
     It is a sacred jacket made of your own shoulders
     As we go over the burning mountain

          And then we stand and watch this whole cold length of time.

FAMILY SHRUB IN THE WOMAN'S MIND AS SHE CONNECTS THESE PEOPLE THROUGH IDLE THINKING

In the upper part of the dome
memory drifts up in obsessive paint:

      birthday in a classroom, little soap operas
      of springtime leaves, climbed the wave of the green
      lawn, stood on the pedals up the immense hill,
      hair is shorn, there is a land of water and music

The earth a great round fruit thrown off the branch

    breaking apart many windows of the cocoon, shape of
    collarbone spreading a drowner bird

    Bathing scraper to remove dirt and oil
        hair suspended in revolving dirt in the lake
        complete sets of bathing tools found in many graves.

Eventually the light goes out on wet oil;
reflection of the painter's face on the paint dries up,
seals her out.

I would like to work in the sun
    sad-dead, you are working with rags
    so sad so sad I do not know what to do
    working with oily rags with beautiful shapes
    I would go see Nana on the boat through
        the oil pattern on the cotton wave

    our light cloth tent
    strung about the dark-boned trees

and campfire, outer branches as ceremonial wreath of innocence

            about the center of their own burning.

I SEND OUT AN ISOSCELES
TRIANGLE TO THE BIRDS AND FISH

Lightning of Bone Struck Blood

Will becomes alive and every second
Mouth waters like a lake for the fish, my sleeves are wet,
my hands rake the dust from things, turn dirty things over.
I tie on a maiden spirit mask:
I am a ceremonial door,
wear a look-downer and spy the yellow fish,
tell the future at dusk.

My animal—tame as a knife.

A girl says, "There is a wheel
                 in my heart."

In younger times the tree
showed a tail we called snake.

My grandfather the mountain as perpetual gray fire.

BIRTHDAY

Walking and braiding roses at once, I took a fall
        upon the flint in my pocket
        and went quietly to the grasses
        to begin a pencil drawing.

I do not know if this will work I hope this will work.

Those who run things perched upon
        the bicycle stutters two earths to go across
        the earth is flat.

Fire a heat rider upon a single hill rider can you see
        the animals from there.
        Fire, extinct animal, solo muscle
        face in the tapestry.

THIS IS DRYING SLOWLY

I snap off one hair from the paintbrush
                          one hair from the tail of a horse
and use it to paint the lashes on this one's face.

In the Family Tree of Trees Ropes Hang on the Arms

Oh, Love, you are moss-backed
everyone age after age
arrives to watch you shower.
See the black brush-strokes of sandal straps
and cuts once lit the blood.

Amourettes, days at the beach, when the weather
sours on the skin of the shore
waves then amplify, oh I do believe
in the three-dimensional implications of the painting
your image loose from the belts of the frame, the face
comes out in the form of a ship

and it is honorable the way you attempt to clean up the waves
with your oar.

GLASS DISPLAY CASE AT THE MUSEUM OF NATURAL HISTORY

Square image and title in the manner
of an ancient Christmas card—

See there a herd of extinct horses
heads low to imaginary ground like white cats
and sunset hills of small camels in death-pose.

The people come in and paint convincing trees.

THE SOUNDS ANIMALS MAKE MEAN THEY ARE PITCHED TO THE HUGE MUSICAL BOX

Plants & Animals

 Amplified with each generation
 flocking up the stairs
 in a beautiful fever of octaves

 We used the old speakers and receiver
 for a chopping block

On our way out with the blood tambourine,
its sad melodic curve a halo punished at your hip

Soundtrack

 There are human sounds between songs or ads
 in the movie theater
 straws rushed with Coke

 The lethargic light of the movie broadcasts human labor,

   actress as skinny and serene as the leg of a deer
   rifle in the swimming pool,
   set to change an image,
   and departure: men who run from one another—
   in fact they are taking their places in an organized sport

Church Choir

The organs act upon the human.
Voice springs up like a guide
amidst the thicket of sound

    edged with poverty
    "He Sends the Rainbow with the Rain"

Driftage of the dream-built trains peeling off so slowly gorgeous
       wild-haired oceans

Homeric quest of American city-block
       goes out like an electric train into landscape
       elevator cables whine, greased with animal fat

Distortion

Candle burns like a drunk mouth, distortion
falls from the amp in piles of pepper
Speech comes out fur-lined
       laughter

Oh airplanist, man-bird, horsewoman—
   listen:
       there is the true horizon;
       there is the artificial horizon.

Music lessons put rain on the lampshade
a halo around each light bulb in the house

True horizon as the folded edge
of sacred sheet music.

THE HAIRLINE CRACK SEE IN THE FOLDED PIECE OF PAPER

Will you lean more on the right side's account of what has happened?
Are you lynched about your spine?
And the deadline of the spine went up in a hurry to bloom
these contrary brains?

I fold the page in half. What is dying on either
side is history.

Is it horrifying running both north and south?

Or what is sinistrorse what is progressive,

It's altimetric lowlihood all the time

long day

The spine climbs its own rungs, gurgles to the brain in babel.

Forget the horrible little bird in the top-hat out there on the post.
Have faith in the ambidextrous scales.

Think on excellent rope work hauling up gorgeous buckets.
A figure is founded in the flagpole of desire.

Your spine is not a steeple which might go
spearing up the godhead.

CONCEPTION IS THE BREAKING CHAIN OF A BURNING TORCH

I Will Indicate These Figures in Light and Shadow

The brain made a branchy crown
and in each weird jewel
a family face
all revolving the handsome
head of God.

Braid as Orderly Tangle of Three Parts

The brooding fire of daylight
His beard was sopping at the stone pool's water.

The first time the animal puts itself into water
or his mother puts him into water

        arranging the fallen leaves into a grove he follows
        the fish backwards and the sea vines smoothing out

        he runs to the chapel and admires the old face
        basket-fishes
        hair looped around the head

It's old in here, in the water.
It is curiosity in our blood
that makes us put the animals in us.

Life Composition: Free Reign of Notes
Yet in the Nest of the Brains

We have to climb out of here
In a different way
From which we first traveled forth

Not vocal chord knotted in cameo—
Death has a song
Bang the orange gong of the sun

Death comes out on the setting scene of Life
Viney on the formal trunks of sonata

Troop sharpening weapon-instruments to drive
The melody forth

Armies swarm in the harpsichord of blood

My right hand hunting melody

The Growth of Ice on Dying Stems

"The name of the bow is life, but its work is death."
                                                                    —Heraclitus

To heal the branch with deathish strokes
green-blue fire of lichen
Death supplies the living branches with shadow-art which falls across
the ground, beneath this wide magnolia and no grass will grow there

Friend-Death clearing out the rocks and living shrubs
to make room for the immortal garden:
the flowers' regeneration is as strong as stone
the lineage of flower-talking is as strong as a mountain

> Green leaves grow thick
> in the cage with the tiger

> In the joust between Life and Death:
> rust is bloodish flowering on the scythe blade

Deathish-lifeish opulence;
Park stocked with game for the hunt—
thorn-branch antler, bait will catch blood

> Spears of rain slant in sparks of light
> torn ivy hanging off the horns
> rainfall hard upon the fawn he is limping

> Water braiding currents in the rapids
> fish within the hood of the wave.

As a breath
ceremonies of fish swirling into the cave
of the Great Death-whale—

pleasure swims in this reservoir
careful strokes through the weedy lake

> The infinite life of fishing the pond on the island
> sound carries across the lifeish–deathish waters

> Gentle Life and Gentle Death
> as they fished upon the water
> in their narrow nighttime boat

SHADOWS GREENING

"The harmonies of the dust storm."
                    —Scott Inguito

Death believes he has achieved non-attachment
          but in truth the leaves about him are romantic
          and they are desirous and fall about him like sunlight as he is covered
          and the centipede is sexual in his stinging expression toward the monk
          in the leaves of the living-dying cave

Larger masculine structures, formidable rosy arms
of the old empress, Life
with the floral drawing across
the castle of a dying tree torn in half

                    Death puts little life-novels in tomb-piles
               and natural ornamentation, aggressive, gentle stuff
               dandelions spotting, mosses banding and frilling, life alights to
                                        loricate the death-pile

CEREMONIAL

Like an upturned cornucopia, a hat on my flowery head
and the torch of my perfume bottle

The life of the town or castle is an upright birthday

    With death's fretsaw
    we may see the view is rendered
    intricate
    and through the openwork of this past century

        it's greened, it's ruined
        braided minerals on the cave walls
        I went into the cave
        of my own consciousness
        and painted animals on the rounds and ledges there
        I am standing or crouching on the shelf of the cave there in
        the mind

            I am The Neanderthal Kings
            with this sweaty ash and jeweled eye

An animal tied to her shade—
studied by my shelter
the territory I mark becomes my cage

        I put this all into the bruised waters of my thoughtfulness
        and white ships moved through the darker chambers

LIFE AND DEATH SING AROUND THE CAMPFIRE

Pomp and trill of flames trickling over the rocks
kiln, firing the vases we fill with cut life,
column breeding heat, Oh tree—

>   do you worry someday your young branches
>   will be on fire for me?

Prince-Death:

>   Hands painted red all but the thumbnail—
>   I pull the reins to my chin and scream and whistle at the same time
>   The rays of my campfire make the trees grow!
>   And red leaves fall over me in drunkard blood.

LIFE AND DEATH AT THE PORTCULLIS

Life and Death at the portcullis
wreaths on either side,
living-dying wreaths
yellow fir reposing as new flowers
aging lanterns to shine in the eyes of Death
hungry symmetry of wreaths is expressive, deathish

The asymmetrical is infinite
climbing with uneven arms
Life follows it, dreading

Symmetry is halting Life on either side of the threshold

BEHEADING THE STATUE PLACES AN IMPORTANT BOOK ON THE SHELF UPSIDE DOWN

Death, your hand against the grain of fur
You are safe as a tiger

> Courtly love, a fly at each wrist
> Old roses mourn as shriveled snouts of horses
>
> And before we were born we were dead
> O, eternal death—
>
> Shall we not love this great ancestor?
> O, death is eternal
>
> My dish, an animal skull
>   Look look the bone in the throat of fruit

Death senses Death painted in Life
Salt on the animal vellum

You upbraid
the slender and evil painting
of life in a terrarium

> Evil light in the yellow oil
> and the dark green trees
> it is a cracked landscape scene
> with a tiny chip fallen out of the center

As he hunts he is enraptured
by the scent of the wound
in the animal track

Life, predatorial, perfumey, enticing with grace
the animalness of the Lady of the Witness

prince-death: naïve, fulfilling his confidence in his own life

      and boats pulled smartly over the flat edge of the earth

ROMANCE

Where will I meet you?

On top of the hill

May I rest there?

So long as the branches are thorny enough to fix your soft nest
      in place.

I will find the animal and carve him up expertly
And I will walk about with a halo of gnats in the hot meadow

      Nose bent wood with a cherry blossom chopping off
      Toenails with stripes of dirt
      Bleating little fruits on the trees
      Bridle, cracked leather and metal, warm and cold

He went to wash her cheeks and nose from the silver basin

EARLY MARRIAGE-SONG OF LIFE AND DEATH

The scarf smells like tears

"I want to break everything around you
because it is you I love especially,
you as Life shining forth."

Her cheeks lit up like rosy lamps

"Thin golden strands on your blessed head
        could be strings in a mythical instrument
        may I pluck them and pull them?"

    Death, sawing at your harp
        or pulling the weedy harp strings
        or pulling the blue-eyed grasses
        or small flowers
        plucking invisible flowers from the harp strings

Life, You Are Death's Amulet

"Now droops the milk-white peacock like a ghost,
   And like a ghost she glimmers on to me."

                                        —Tennyson

You are the tilted picture in her labor
you are presented
as a new face

             Bleeding like a lighthouse
             in its solitary, virginal burning

   Oh little child—
             a bouquet of blood
             of the family,
             a photograph of the first fire

Death interprets the speech of his children,
   girlhood, the porch light feels elemental

       these golden living leaves
       are celebrated
       everything made for them to be made upon

As the rays of color imbricate from the peacock's tail

The death-braid a bridge over the lifeish ravine

             Underworld, yellow roots of grass go into it, gypsyish

DEATH AND LIFE
AS SNODGRASS AND CLEO
EQUALING THE LOVE POEMS
OF SNODGRASS AND CLEO

Cleo Peering Through the Deathesque Cutwork

Through cuts in her fan's boned-pleats Cleo will witness—

The whirlpool with its ferocious, scrubbed center

Tongue in its small hut
gills look like tightly folded cloth
cold air tastes bright like salt

Our lanterns, stone cups filled with burning reindeer fat
rock-volume, swells of gut and hip on the cave wall, animal

Fire crushes the ladder of the tree
half the wood rotting with bugs and earth and clover,
half of it rotting into the fire

Slaughtering the animal
was like freeing him with a knife
from a little trap—

Sawing at the little rope
that held its neck to its mortality

CLEO AND CLEO

Dusk and high summer, and the street lamps
lit up just as the family Duesenberg rolled past.
The steely hood ornament is the 1783 B.C. Head of an Official
The lace on my cap sleeves like pianoey fingers.

SNODGRASS AND SNODGRASS

Firmly piano, breaking low tables
Of hushed golden music

SNODGRASS AND CLEO'S CONCEPT "LAND"

The snapping sound of roots pulled from the earth
wouldn't do, so we keep our heads tilted together in bed
and let thoughts of the land build up between them
These are little roots stitched through the forehead

Snodgrass and Cleo make translations of the animals
(but first Cleo has a scary memory of Kentucky:

    Was it like the distances between human animals which are spaces
        between blood?
    I will put a sculpture in my painting
        names scratched into the base
    Here was a statue put up for blood, and taken down for the blood
        of the living:
    The slaughterhouse wall in Covington was dragged out of the old
        neighborhood
    The blood-earth around the old wall needed three years to dry
        before we could build something new.
    I am thinking on The Holy Family with Deer.
    This earth is not a mystery, but I am a mystery to myself.)

Though she was filled with light
there was a light shining out at her from the old house

    beardy vines
    chandeliers of darkness

"We're camping out
In the lights"

Concept Land, II:
Snodgrass dreams about an owl—

Owl

A germ turning with its pretty edges in space
And hard and strong, like a tree given eyes
Face seems the two dimensional entrapment of the blind
The stillness and symmetry of Egyptian art
Eyes retreat beyond the scene of the body

The sea braids the temperatures through mixed woods
The pilgrimage is not austere but lush
Plumage of the hilly trill
The heavy horse is snorting but then he is chewing roses

The first part is tying ribbons on the horse
The second part is the horse
Accents develop in the animals

Childhood chants, Indian chants

Played on the piano in adulthood
An expert is past adulthood
Wet the dust and fashion it, dust falling into blood
The fire is frozen in that it is contained
Frozen things burst, fiery things burst

Pumping water from the garden out
Air is spotted, it is dark in the woods

CLEO AS THE CONTESSA

There are so many cities upon
the hills
with the white buildings
and square windows

Little thousand
Little thousand

Often in sunnier times
I was born unto another lady
that lady was Myself,
and within her liver and within her idea and countenance
I lived within the heart of the Contessa

> The Dangerous Crystal Mountain, Water on the Cloth Is Death, This Is
> an Abandoned Ski Path

> And lowered the grey set

> In this way it was
> shadow as reflection.

(Count pushed into the burgundy wave from the boat
and we were traveling to New York. The water's surface
curls as it boils, those slopes were laughless,
the tallest mountain in the world which you can view from space.)

I found her, myself, walking down the hallway of the ship
white white teeth and a golden cane
dominoes laden with little diamond circles
To Snodgrass she didn't know Snodgrass and he was therefore
a created man
That is becoming to you, I said to her and myself
and all her feathers were lit up by the fire

Monsters swimming back and forth in green swimming pools
I said give me fifteen more years
Though she never laughed and never spoke
and certainly never spoke with laughter
It was like a child's hospital operation to become this woman
and how wonderful to feel so grave
My clothes became tapestries
with leopards and green mountains all over them

And I departed from her, like a small boat from a big ship
And like plankton and like sugar

How slow a minute like the slow depth of the Indian Ocean

The Contessa as a Snail

First I must tell you
Her, the Contessa,
I, the former "sweaty peasant head,"
had become, and now lived in the castle in New York
which was 113th street and strange,
fire building up in my parlor
making the snow melt in the city.
This white building with black ironwork
a bedroom which was Olympic-sized, war-field sized,
and in my mahogany bed only one light could be seen and that was
the eternal mini-sun of my cigarette, never went out and lit the
                    next one and so forth

Silent.

Never needing to address the assistant
who wheels out the black and white television and knows to keep the volume
Loud so that the little speaker shakes in the static
That '70s Show he wheels it in just in time for the Big Star song
and it nearly breaks my eardrums.
My eyes are solemn and spooky and I often see myself
in the "yes" of twins.

Heading out on a train to Boston,
telescope, trunk and a miniature horse made of diamonds,
I take a bath and pretend I am a whale with an encasing indigo beard.
I know The Poor will come home
and tv is their pile of millisecond jewels
turning and flashing in the light.

But, lo,

I dropped from this grand life in my apartment-castle
to the life of this garden-thing,
and now slip down black glass
and am wound up infinitely in harshness and softness
and I rest in the rain within this skull
and I have become a lock,
a lock which is a music box of silence
and I wave my skins infinitely on the patio floor.

The servants do not know where I have gone;
the earth will serve me now
and all of the fragments of ferns and the tiny fragment of space I live
within. I stay clear of the ants and feel that I am all hunger.
I could have become a snake and let my stripes flash out like notebook
paper with masculine writing
but this snail I have become has such a quiet shell-skull.

I am not a god, but the god of my own mind.

ALL RIGHT! SNODGRASS MAKES CLEO A PRESENT

Tralala Snodgrass fashioned Cleo a beautiful mahogany trumpet
when she played it her spittle formed glass beads on the wood.
Not a seamstress whose fingers are taped with bandages as she mellows a
rip in her mistress' silks, but joyously
she was singing and playing in the music.

MMM HMMM, TV NIGHT

All the televisions of the world made like these little banners
with good necking and sweaty checkered dresses and tv booze—

It was such a little thing to see the whole movie of your life
on this diminutive Sony, but it was pretty awesome to watch such a
special from an historic house in a springtime rain.

I had this tight skirt on last night and scooted around in these tall
boots but now I am in an old thin nightgown like I'm sandy clover,
and I am personally thanking you, Snodgrass, for these quiet times
between the waves of heavy make-out sessions and interpreting Cezanne
on the piano.

If I were a country singer before I was born
there would be a movie on tv about me right now called "Legacy"
and the family would have seen an earlier screening in uncomfy tights,
violence like the frosted edges of my beer mug
holding up the gold—

It was a sad song.
Someone could have torn me apart saying,

Cleo
O you're just an old
kitten

So see I am glad it's not a big deal kind of night
it's nice just to scratch my armpit and go get a sparkling water
during the commercials.

OK, Snodgrass and Cleo Try Out Indian Drums Called Tabla

The instrument was blue library-book rain
We have let loose the drapery of sunlight

Nothing could anger me now

There are microbes and small atoms with their feelings
The hot mouth of the wolf pup as he eats up the fresh kill
This song which is the measure of my body in the lake
Reflect on these themes and then imagine the colored strings dragging
lightly
from each

IN THE PARVIS THE GREEN WREATH REASSEMBLED

ALL THE BUILDINGS HAVE GROWN OUT OF THIS ONE GARDEN

I.

The Christmas tree of lights has blown over.

    All the members of this family are on separate ladders.
    The identity is perpendicular to the plane.

A zoo is built of modified classical columns
    where young families shyly approach the smell of urine.
    The zoo is the place of the grey and gold drum.

    Aerial photograph of this graveyard
    instructs urban planning. The miniature city
    grows monuments oiled by the hands of the public.

Wind moves the fan on the cold porch, the hairs on her arms move
in a slow march. There is the belt you tied around the snowheap, who is
saying, My silence is my power, bullying me.

II.

This is where you were born, and there are playing fields now.

Your music is the light in the center of this static rain.
Carafe on the table to water the flowers of drinking. A young girl or
animal paws her way though family albums, shadows crack away from the fruit,
lake water drinks up the old airplane.

Here is the first fire, and a fire is an infant upon a horse.

III.

The harp of reruns at nighttime. The animals of lights
will chew off your hair, or put white hair on your head in a pile
of bones.

But darling look at this picture: you are the head
of a headless tree, or this one: the husband and wife
transport the beggar on their boat
who then reveals himself to be Christ.

DEVOTIONAL

The lock on the door as grace note, come inside please
    and rest your face in hands.
All winter, a devotional in the house of the ancestor
    printed I Love This Living in orange stripes
    and put the paper into the battery hull of an ancient flashlight—
The white light spots the house and the surrounding field
    where small boys could jump and sink into silos of grain.

Melvin and Garland were sleeping in the room next to the kitchen
    we went in and they had their heads covered up,
    the ceiling was bad, snow was falling on the bed
    like a faith curist. Papa combed ice from his hair,
    and the wine glass full of water froze on the mantle.
What appears on the outside of the glass, the grease from your hand
    leaves the tail of a bird

A Blackboard of Motions

Flowers twitching on horizontal rows
Fire as a little light with a string tied to a stick

Circular white fence encloses the pasture
for a white horse
who will one day vanish, and the field grass will grow tall
tall within the circle

HARMONY

New branches of the tree
tap out into the air
in little marks
like a blind man
making his way upstairs

KIND SPACE

We are drinking warm rings of saké, the country light
yaws about the lake.
The city light shines past the inward man.
Mother sighs, "The city is our cumulative fear of the dark."
Father, if the blood ends at your fist,
you are only holding tightly to a lantern.
Sticks of wintertime lightning
dropped felt leaves all around the cabin.
Chirping spaces between leaves.

Kind space, move back—
Conforming to the shape of growing things

FAIR

Grief-man, look here the open forest doors
frame a ribcage of mystical forest light
the march of blood from the heart in enormous beauty:
here come the brides.

For the ponies, fields of roses are hundreds of pink lollipops.
Lady's got shiny hair and over the fur collar of her coat,
the bells have a pretty fever.

Hose water shines against the windows
the young children are laughing at the water soundlessly
they are flocks of suns in the old eye of a horse.

THE INVENTION OF REPETITION IS A KIND OF HARMONY

So many pilgrims have kissed the feet of this statue the feet have worn
away

I fall asleep praying; I go on
praying as the long line of light which trains us
keeps ringing out into the hereafter.

    A statue inside sleep,
       sororal right hand to left hand
       raised in the art of re-attaching fallen
           notes of early plums—
                       whole notes of rest which
                       chopped themselves
                            from the staff of trees.

The invention of repetition is a kind of harmony

       Consider the hollow pulse in each stone stair,
                   public processions,
                   and public processions upon water

    My hands part in their sleeping doors

        I am opening your sleep to locate the white marker.

The Dying Arrangement as a Living Being

It is dying and animate
                              to direct light, or to create privacy

the passage, musical and something too to follow with the eye
        in the lovely dying arrangement, grasses and lights forming the hut

                    a living death
            the way we admire art, not this only-death

    but the taking apart of anything, this is living

                    material

a 1723 earthquake happened solely in a forest
            with no human despair of buildings
                decorum to the event meant a whole flock of leaves coming up
            just the odd branch of a clutching jaw
        and the goldish blood on the living trees not pollenous dust
                    washing is kill
                    and let-breath

the dying arrangement is a living being

Notes

[p.22] *Dish with Peaches and Bats*, porcelain, Qing dynasty.

[p.33] Hymn "Madonna, You Are More Beautiful than Sunshine" composed by Robert Katscher; hymn "Standing on the Promises" composed by Russell Kelso Carter.

[p.47] Hymn "He Sends the Rainbow with the Rain" (composer unknown).

[p.56] Heraclitus, Fragment LXVI, from *The Fragments of the Work of Heraclitus of Ephesus on Nature*.

[p.58] Scott Inguito, "Praise with Squirrels."

[p.66] Alfred, Lord Tennyson, "Now Sleeps the Crimson Petal."

[p.72] *Head of an Official*, stone sculpture, Egypt, 1783 B.C.

[p.74] *Holy Family with Deer*, Rodolphe Bresdin.

The Madeleine P. Plonsker Emerging Writer's Residency Prize

Jessica Savitz
2009 Winner (Poetry)

Gretchen E. Henderson
2010 Winner (Prose)

Each spring, Lake Forest College, in conjunction with &NOW Books, sponsors an emerging writer under forty years old who has no major book publication. This writer spends two months in residence at our campus in Chicago's northern suburbs on the shore of Lake Michigan. There are no formal teaching duties attached to the residency. Time is to be spent completing a manuscript, participating in the annual Lake Forest Literary Festival, and offering a series of public presentations.

The completed manuscript will be published (upon approval) by &NOW Books with distribution by Northwestern University Press.

The stipend is $10,000 with a housing suite and campus meals provided by the college.

In odd years we accept applications in poetry and cross/mixed/undefinable genres.
In even years we accept applications in prose and cross/mixed/undefinable genres.

Yearly postmark deadline, April 1.

Please send:
1) Curriculum vitae
2) No more than 30 pages of manuscript in progress
3) A one-page statement of plans for completion

Plonsker Residency
Department of English
Lake Forest College
Box A16
555 N. Sheridan Road
Lake Forest, IL 60045.

Direct inquiries to andnow@lakeforest.edu with the subject line: Plonsker Prize.